by Iain Gray

Lang**Syne**

PUBLISHING

WRITING *to* REMEMBER

WRITING *to* REMEMBER

79 Main Street, Newtongrange,
Midlothian EH22 4NA
Tel: 0131 344 0414   Fax: 0845 075 6085
E-mail: info@lang-syne.co.uk
www.langsyneshop.co.uk

Design by Dorothy Meikle
Printed by Ricoh Print Scotland
© Lang Syne Publishers Ltd 2015

ISBN 978-1-85217-420-0

Finlay

MOTTO:
A noble heart is an immovable heart
(and) Brave in difficulties.

CREST:
The head of a boar
(and) A hand clutching a sword.

NAME variations include:
Findlay
Findlaw
Findlow
Finlayson
Finley

The spirit of the clan means
much to thousands of people

Chapter one:

The origins of the clan system

by Rennie McOwan

The original Scottish clans of the Highlands and the great families of the Lowlands and Borders were gatherings of families, relatives, allies and neighbours for mutual protection against rivals or invaders.

Scotland experienced invasion from the Vikings, the Romans and English armies from the south. The Norman invasion of what is now England also had an influence on land-holding in Scotland. Some of these invaders stayed on and in time became 'Scottish'.

The word clan derives from the Gaelic language term 'clann', meaning children, and it was first used many centuries ago as communities were formed around tribal lands in glens and mountain fastnesses.

The format of clans changed over the centuries, but at its best the chief and his family held the land on behalf of all, like trustees, and the ordinary clansmen and women believed they had a blood relationship with the founder of their clan.

There were two way duties and obligations. An inadequate chief could be deposed and replaced by someone of greater ability.

Clan people had an immense pride in race. Their relationship with the chief was like adult children to a father and they had a real dignity.

The concept of clanship is very old and a more feudal notion of authority gradually crept in.

Pictland, for instance, was divided into seven principalities ruled by feudal leaders who were the strongest and most charismatic leaders of their particular groups.

By the sixth century the 'British' kingdoms of Strathclyde, Lothian and Celtic Dalriada (Argyll) had emerged and Scotland, as one nation, began to take shape in the time of King Kenneth MacAlpin.

Some chiefs claimed descent from ancient kings which may not have been accurate in every case.

By the twelfth and thirteenth centuries the clans and families were more strongly brought under the central control of Scottish monarchs.

Lands were awarded and administered more and more under royal favour, yet the power of the area clan chiefs was still very great.

The long wars to ensure Scotland's

independence against the expansionist ideas of English monarchs extended the influence of some clans and reduced the lands of others.

Those who supported Scotland's greatest king, Robert the Bruce, were awarded the territories of the families who had opposed his claim to the Scottish throne.

In the Scottish Borders country – the notorious Debatable Lands – the great families built up a ferocious reputation for providing warlike men accustomed to raiding into England and occasionally fighting one another.

Chiefs had the power to dispense justice and to confiscate lands and clan warfare produced a society where martial virtues – courage, hardiness, tenacity – were greatly admired.

Gradually the relationship between the clans and the Crown became strained as Scottish monarchs became more orientated to life in the Lowlands and, on occasion, towards England.

The Highland clans spoke a different language, Gaelic, whereas the language of Lowland Scotland and the court was Scots and in more modern times, English.

Highlanders dressed differently, had different

customs, and their wild mountain land sometimes seemed almost foreign to people living in the Lowlands.

It must be emphasised that Gaelic culture was very rich and story-telling, poetry, piping, the clarsach (harp) and other music all flourished and were greatly respected.

Highland culture was different from other parts of Scotland but it was not inferior or less sophisticated.

Central Government, whether in London or Edinburgh, sometimes saw the Gaelic clans as a challenge to their authority and some sent expeditions into the Highlands and west to crush the power of the Lords of the Isles.

Nevertheless, when the eighteenth century Jacobite Risings came along the cause of the Stuarts was mainly supported by Highland clans.

The word Jacobite comes from the Latin for James – Jacobus. The Jacobites wanted to restore the exiled Stuarts to the throne of Britain.

The monarchies of Scotland and England became one in 1603 when King James VI of Scotland (1st of England) gained the English throne after Queen Elizabeth died.

The Union of Parliaments of Scotland and England, the Treaty of Union, took place in 1707.

Some Highland clans, of course, and Lowland families opposed the Jacobites and supported the incoming Hanoverians.

After the Jacobite cause finally went down at Culloden in 1746 a kind of ethnic cleansing took place. The power of the chiefs was curtailed. Tartan and the pipes were banned in law.

Many emigrated, some because they wanted to, some because they were evicted by force. In addition, many Highlanders left for the cities of the south to seek work.

Many of the clan lands became home to sheep and deer shooting estates.

But the warlike traditions of the clans and the great Lowland and Border families lived on, with their descendants fighting bravely for freedom in two world wars.

Remember the men from whence you came, says the Gaelic proverb, and to that could be added the role of many heroic women.

The spirit of the clan, of having roots, whether Highland or Lowland, means much to thousands of people.

*Clan warfare produced a society where courage
and tenacity were greatly admired*

Chapter two:

On the fields of conflict

Derived from what was the popular Gaelic personal name *Fionnlagh*, meaning 'fair hero' or 'blond warrior', the surname of Finlay and its popular variations that include Finlayson and Finley, has been present in Scotland from earliest times.

Ranked at 96 in the list of the 100 most popular surnames in Scotland, it is not identified with any region in particular.

One of the earliest records of the name, in one of its now redundant forms, concerns a Stirlingshire landowner, Brice Fynlawesone, one of the signatories to the Ragman Roll of 1296.

Scotland had been thrown into crisis ten years before this date, with the death of Alexander II and the death four years later of his successor, the Maid of Norway, who died while en route to Scotland to take up the crown.

John Balliol was enthroned at Scone as King of Scots in 1292. Fatefully for the nation the ambitious

Edward I of England had been invited to arbitrate in the bitter dispute over the succession to the throne, and the hapless Balliol was Edward's chosen man.

The Scots rose in revolt against the imperialist designs of the English king in July of 1296 but, living up to his reputation of 'Hammer of the Scots', he brought the entire nation under his subjugation little less than a month later, garrisoning strategic locations throughout the length and breadth of the nation.

To reinforce his domination of Scotland, 1,500 earls, bishops, burgesses and other landowners were required to sign a humiliating treaty of fealty, known as the Ragman Roll, because of the number of ribbons that dangled from the seals of the reluctant signatories.

It is on this document that the name of Brice Fynlawesone is found – indicating that by this period he was judged as being in the higher ranks of Scottish society.

Later records of the name include a Duncan Finlayson, recorded in Banff in 1342, and Thom Findlaisone, in Dunkeld, more than 185 years later.

Although a number of family Coats of Arms are attributed to the Finlays, they are also entitled, as a sept, or sub-branch, of Clan Farquharson, to assume the motto, crest and tartan of this proud clan.

Tracing a descent from the Farquharson Chiefs and, as such, kinsfolk of the clan, whose name is derived from 'fear' and 'char', indicating 'dear one', the Finlays shared for centuries in both their fortunes and misfortunes.

With their motto of "Fidelity and fortitude" and crest of a demi-lion holding a sword in its right paw, the Farquharsons take their name, known in Gaelic as *Mac Fhearchair*, from Farquhar Shaw, a son of Alexander Mackintosh of Rothiemurchus, the 5th Chief of Clan Shaw, and whose territory lay in the Braes of Mar, in Deeside.

It was after his son married Isobel Stewart, the heiress of Invercauld, near Braemar, that the chiefly line of the Farquharsons became more properly known as the Farquharsons of Invercauld.

Invercauld House remains the seat of the Clan Chief of the Farquharsons.

Farquhar Shaw's grandson, Finla Mor Farquharson, along with many of his clan and kinsfolk such as the Finlays, were among those killed in 1547 in the battle of Pinkie, near Musselburgh, on Scotland's east coast.

The battle had followed the invasion of a 25,000-strong English army under the Duke of

Somerset, and 3,000 clansmen and their kinsmen under the leadership of the Earl of Argyll were either killed on the battlefield or forced to flee to safety.

Nearly 50 years after the battle, the Farquharsons and their kinsfolk entered a bond with Clan Mackintosh, thus making them, along with others that included the Christies, MacPhersons, MacThomases of Finegand and the Davidsons, members of the mighty confederation of clans known as Clan Chattan.

As members of Clan Chattan – whose motto is "Touch not the cat without a glove", and crest a rampant wildcat, the Farquharsons and their kinsfolk such as the Finlays were loyal in their support of the Royal House of Stewart.

Following the "Glorious Revolution" of 1688 that brought William of Orange and his wife Mary to the thrones of England and Scotland, John Graham of Claverhouse, Viscount Dundee, raised the Royal Standard in favour of the exiled Stewart monarch James VII and II.

Gathering a 2,500-strong force of clansmen that included a contingent under John Farquharson of Inverey, he engaged a 4000-strong government force under General Hugh Mackay of Scourie at the Pass of Killiecrankie on July 27, 1689.

Brave, but undisciplined, the clansmen fired off a volley of musket fire before throwing the muskets to the ground and rushing pell-mell down hill into Mackay's closely packed ranks.

The clansmen were mown down in hundreds by the disciplined musket fire of Mackay's troopers, but not before inflicting equally heavy losses.

Both sides suffered terribly in the battle, with John Farquharson among the many dead, and the outcome proved to be inconclusive – while John Graham of Claverhouse died the next day from his wounds.

In the following century, the Farquharsons and their Finlay kinsmen also fought for the cause of the Stewarts in the abortive Jacobite Risings of 1715 and 1745.

Bearers of the name have gained distinction, far from their native lands, on different fields of battle.

Born in 1893 in Guardsbridge, Fife, David Finlay was a Scottish recipient of the Victoria Cross (V.C), the highest award for bravery in the face of enemy action for British and Commonwealth forces.

He had been a lance-corporal in the Black Watch (Royal Highlanders) during the First World War when, in May of 1915 near Rue de Bois, France, he led a bombing party of 12 men against an enemy emplacement.

All but three, including Finlay, escaped death or injury during a vicious counter-attack and Finlay, ordering the other two to crawl back to safety, assisted one of his wounded comrades by carrying him 100 yards back to their own lines. Promoted to sergeant, he was killed in action less than a year later in Mesopotamia, now present day Iraq.

His V.C. is on display at the Black Watch Museum, Balhouse Castle, Fife.

Yet another Scottish recipient of the V.C. during the First World War was George de Cardonnel Findlay, born in 1889 in Balloch, Loch Lomondside.

Commissioned into the Royal Engineers, he won the Military Cross for gallantry at the battle of Passchendaele in August of 1917.

Promoted to the rank of major in the 409 (Lowland) Field Company, Corps of Royal Engineers, he won his V.C. in November of 1918 by leading an assault party that, despite heavy enemy fire, managed to bridge the Sambre-Oise Canal south of Catillon.

Later achieving the rank of colonel, he died in 1967, after having served for a time as Deputy Lord Lieutenant of Dumbarton.

His V.C. is on display at the Royal Engineers Museum, Chatham, Kent.

Chapter three:

Blazing trails

Far from the field of battle, bearers of the Finlay name, in all its popular spelling variations, have made their mark on history through a colourful range of more peaceful endeavours.

One particularly pioneering bearer of the name was the Canadian explorer and fur trader Jacques Finlay, also known as Jacco Finlay, born in 1768.

Employed for a time with the North West Company, he not only established a number of fur trading posts, but also blazed the trail across the Rockies that, in 1807, greatly aided the English-born explorer David Thompson in his crossing of the Continental Divide.

Finlay, who died in 1828, is also credited with having contributed to Thompson's discovery of the Columbia River.

Credited as having introduced the Industrial Revolution to Finland, James Finlayson was the engineer and businessman born in 1772 in Glasgow.

Moving to St Petersburg, Russia, in 1817, the

Scot founded a textile factory in an enterprise that had the backing of Tsar Alexander I.

Also with the Tsar's approval, Finlayson, a devout adherent of the Quaker religious faith, visited Finland – then under Russian rule – to sell Bibles, returning in 1820 along with his wife, Margaret, to build a factory in the town of Tampere.

Utilising water power from the Tammerkosk river, the factory made machinery for the textile industry while, before his death in 1852, he also established a number of cotton mills.

From nineteenth century Finland to nineteenth century Scotland, John Ritchie Findlay was the newspaper owner and noted philanthropist who was born in 1824 in Arbroath, Angus.

Following the failure of his father's drapery business in 1842, he found employment in Edinburgh in the offices of the *Scotsman* – the newspaper that had been co-founded and later wholly owned by his great-uncle, John Ritchie.

Becoming a partner in the firm in 1868 and inheriting a majority stake following his great-uncle's death two years later, he is recognised today as having been instrumental in increasing the newspaper's circulation and influence.

He also enjoyed a considerable increase in his personal wealth, large sums of which he spent on public benefactions.

These included, at a cost of more than £70,000, the Scottish National Portrait Gallery, opened in Edinburgh in 1889, while he also contributed much of his own art collection to the National Gallery of Scotland.

Having refused the offer of a baronetcy in 1896, the unassuming philanthropist died two years later.

One of his sons, James Leslie Findlay, did in later life accept a baronetcy – an honour bestowed not only because of his proprietorship of the *Scotsman*, but also because of his distinguished career as an architect.

Born in 1888, he served in France during the First World War as Lieutenant Colonel in command of the First Lowland Brigade of the Royal Field Artillery, before being invalided out.

A founder, along with James Bow Dunn, of the Edinburgh architectural firm Dunn and Findlay, his greatest architectural achievement before his death in 1952 was the *Scotsman* building in the capital's North Bridge, and which, having been renovated in recent years, functions today as The Scotsman Hotel.

From Scotland to Canada, James Findlay was the Ontario newspaper owner and politician who was born of Scottish stock in 1833 in Chateauguay, Lower Canada.

Owner and editor of the *Pembroke Observer*, he was also a Liberal Member of the Canadian House of Commons from 1873 to 1874; he died in 1923.

Also in Ontario, Hugh Finlayson was the businessman and politician born in Edinburgh in 1810.

Immigrating to North America at the age of 22 from his native Scotland, he settled for a time in New York City before moving to Paris, Ontario, working as a harness and saddle maker and operating his own tannery.

Entering politics, he served as mayor of Paris in 1858 and, as a Liberal, served in the Legislative Assembly of Ontario from 1867 until 1879; he died in 1889.

From Canada to New Zealand, Martyn Finlay, born in 1912 and who died in 1999, was the noted lawyer and Labour Party politician who served as president of the party from 1969 to 1978 and as Attorney General and Minister of Justice from 1972 to 1975.

In the contemporary politics of New Zealand, Chris Finlayson, born in 1956, is the lawyer and

National Party politician who has also held the post of Attorney General, in addition to that of Minister for Arts, Culture and Heritage.

Chairperson from 1998 to 2001 of Creative New Zealand's Arts Board, he has also served as a trustee of the New Zealand Symphony Orchestra.

In British politics, Robert Finlay, born in 1842 in Newhaven, Edinburgh, and who was later created 1st Viscount Finlay, was the lawyer and politician who served as Lord Chancellor of Great Britain from 1916 to 1919.

Also elected a judge of the Permanent Court of International Justice, established by the League of Nations following the end of the First World War, he died in 1929.

From politics to the realms of religion, Hugh Findlay was the far-travelled Mormon missionary who was born in 1822 in Newmilns, East Ayrshire.

Baptised at the age of 26 into the faith of The Church of Jesus Christ of Latter Day Saints, as the Mormons are more properly known, from 1851 to 1855 he carried out the first Mormon missionary work in India.

This was undertaken along with William Willes and, later, his younger brother Allan Findlay.

Settling with his wife in Riverdale, Utah, and later in Salt Lake City, he set off on his missionary work once again in 1878.

His destination this time was the Shetland Islands, off the northern coast of his native Scotland, and where he spent two years before returning to America.

It was here, in Fish Haven, Idaho, that he died at the age of 77.

From missionary work to meteorology, John Park Finley was the U.S. Army Signal Service officer and meteorologist credited with having been the first to make intensive studies of tornadoes.

Born in 1854 in Ann Arbor, Michigan, he wrote the first book on the natural phenomena, set up the first nationwide weather observer networks in the United States and opened the first aviation weather school.

He died in 1943, by which time many of his meteorological forecasting techniques were being put to vital use by the Allied forces engaged in the Second World War.

Chapter four:

On the world stage

Awarded a CBE in 1984 for services to acting, Frank Finlay is the veteran English actor of stage, television and film who was born in 1926 in Farnworth, Lancashire.

A devout Roman Catholic and a member of the British Catholic Stage Guild, the numerous stage plays in which he has acted include *Hamlet*, *Mother Courage*, *Juno and the Paycock* and *The Crucible*, while from 1958 to 1959 he was on Broadway for the acclaimed *Epitaph for George Dillon*.

Television roles have included *Casanova* in the BBC series of that name, while he is also known for his role as Adolf Hitler in the 1972 *The Death of Adolf Hitler*.

His role of Iago in the 1965 film *Othello* won him an Academy Award nomination for Best Supporting Actor, as did his performance in the 2002 *The Pianist*.

Other films in which he has starred include the 1968 *Shoes of the Fisherman*, the 1973 *The Three Musketeers* and, from 2007, *The Waiting Room*.

Playing roles in more than 33 Laurel and Hardy films, **James Finlayson**, also known as Jimmy Finlayson, was the Scottish actor who was born in Larbert, Stirlingshire, in 1887 and who died in 1953.

Dropping out of his studies at Edinburgh University to pursue a career in acting, his first main role was in the London West End stage production of *Bunty Pulls the Strings*.

Immigrating to the United States in 1912 and reprising his West End role on Broadway, he later headed for Hollywood, where he appeared in a number of Mack Sennett comedies, including as one of the Keystone Cops.

Usually cast as a villain in the Laurel and Hardy films, he developed his trademark expression of a long, drawn-out "Dohhhhhh!" when his nefarious schemes were thwarted.

This was adapted in much later times for Homer Simpson, in the television cartoon series *The Simpsons*, as "Doh!"

In contemporary times, **William Finley**, born in 1942 in New York City, is the American actor who has appeared in films that include the 1985 *Double Negative* and the 2006 *The Black Dahlia*.

In the creative world of art, **Ian Hamilton**

Finlay was the multi-accomplished artist, gardener, poet and writer born to Scottish parents in 1925 in Nassau, Bahamas.

Educated at Dollar Academy, near Stirling, he served with the army during the Second World War, later working as a shepherd before turning his hand to short stories and poems while living on the Orkney island of Rousay.

Some of his work, including his 1958 *The Sea Bed and Other Stories* and his 1960 *The Dancers Inherit the Party*, was broadcast by the BBC, while in 1963 he published *Rapel*.

This was his first collection of what he termed 'concrete poetry' – in which the typography and layout of the words on the page contributes to the overall effect.

This technique was developed into the composition of poems inscribed on stone, known as 'poem objects', and features in the garden known as Little Sparta that he and his wife, Sue Finlay, created in the Pentland Hills, near Edinburgh.

The recipient of numerous honours and awards that include the 1985 Turner Prize, the 2002 Scottish Arts Council Creative Scotland Award and honorary doctorates from Aberdeen, Glasgow and Heriot-Watt universities, he died in 2006.

This was two years after a Scotish newspaper poll of artists, art gallery directors and other arts professionals voted Little Sparta as the most important work of Scottish art.

Finlay's enduring legacy of Little Sparta is now preserved with the help of The Little Sparta Trust.

The creator of more than 2,600 works of graphic art throughout his 35-year career, **Virgil Finlay** was the American science fiction, pulp fantasy and horror illustrator born in 1914 in Rochester, New York.

An illustrator for magazines that included *Weird Tales* and *The American Weekly*, he served with the U.S. Army during the Second World War in the Pacific, including through the battle for Okinawa, and also lent his artistic talent to producing morale-boosting posters and illustrations. He died in 1971.

A wildlife photographer and a conservationist, **William Lovell Finley** was born in 1876 in Southern California to parents who had earlier travelled as children by covered wagon from Missouri to California.

His great grandfather, **Asa Finley**, had been the first elected judge of Saline County, Missouri, while his uncle, **William Asa Finley**, was the first president of Oregon State University.

In 1905, Finley and Herman T. Bohlman visited and photographed Tule Lake and Lower Klamath Lake, in the Pacific Southwest Region, and their subsequent report, published and illustrated in *Bird Lore* magazine, led to President Theodore Roosevelt setting the areas aside as Federal bird observatories.

Elected to the board of the National Association of Audubon Societies for the Protection of Wild Birds and Animals – later the National Audubon Society – and also appointed to Oregon's Game Commission, he died in 1953.

The William L. Finley National Wildlife Refuge, on the western edge of the Willamette Valley of Northwestern Oregon, is named in his honour.

Born in 1901, **Harold Finlay** was the New Zealand palaeontologist and conchologist whose work on the study of shells won him a Hector Memorial medal ten years before his death in 1951.

In the world of the written word, Peter Finlay, born in 1961 in Old Reynella, South Australia is the award-winning Australian novelist who writes under the nom-de-plume of **DBC Pierre**.

His first novel, the comic *Vernon God Little*, won the 2003 Booker Prize for Fiction, making him, to date, only the third Australian-born author to be so honoured. The novel also won him a Whitbread First Novel Award, making him the first writer to receive both a Booker and a Whitbread award for the same book.

Resident for some years in the Republic of Ireland, his other works include the 2006 *Ludmilla's Broken English* and the 2009 *Suddenly Doctor Cox*.

Author of the noted *History of Greece*, published in sections between 1843 and 1861, **George Finlay** was the historian who was born to Scottish parents in Faversham, Kent, in 1799.

A friend and contemporary of Lord Byron, and, in common with the great poet, a champion of the cause of Greek independence from Turkey, he died in 1875.

Bearers of the name have also excelled in the highly competitive world of sport.

Nicknamed "Fit Finlay" and "Sir Finlay", **Dave Finlay** is the former Northern Irish semi-professional wrestler who was born in 1958 in Carrickfergus.

Winner of the 1982 British Heavy Middleweight Championship and the World Championship Wrestling title in 1998, he has also worked as a road agent for World Wrestling Entertainment (WWE) and is a former winner of the WWE United States Championship.

Not only a top British athlete but also a Second World War fighter pilot, Group Captain Donald Osborne Finlay, better known as **Don Finlay**, was born in 1909 in Christchurch, Hampshire.

Winner of a bronze medal in the 110-metres hurdles at the 1932 Olympics in Los Angeles, a bronze in the same event at the 1936 Olympics in Berlin and gold at the 1938 European Championships in Paris, he later flew Spitfires during the 1940 Battle of Britain with No. 54 Squadron RAF.

A recipient of the Distinguished Flying Cross, his victory tally for downed enemy planes was four.

Later commander of 906 Wing in Burma, he died in 1970.

In the sport of ice hockey, **Brian Finley**, born in 1981 in Sault Ste. Marie, Ontario is the retired Canadian professional goaltender who played for teams that include the Nashville Predators and the Boston Bruins.

A five-time Golden Glove Award winner, **Steve Finley**, born in 1965 in Union City, Tennessee, is the former Major League baseball outfielder who played for teams that include the Baltimore Oriels, Houston Astros, San Francisco Giants and, in 2007, Colorado Rockies.

Also in baseball, Oscar Finley, also known as Charlie O, but better known as **Charlie Finley**, was the flamboyant American businessman who bought the franchise for the Major League team Oakland Athletics, then located in Kansas City, and later moved it to Oakland in 1968.

Born in 1918 in Ensley, Alabama, he made his fortune in the insurance business and, it was while his baseball team was in Kansas City that he lured the Beatles to play the Kansas City Municipal Stadium – after having promised the citizens of Kansas that he would do so.

This was during the Beatles' first tour of North America in 1964, and Finley persuaded the band to appear after offering $150,000 – at the time the highest fee ever paid for a musical concert.

His many noted stunts included offering his players a $300 bonus to grow a moustache; he died in 1996.

In the sports of rowing and sailing, **Conn Findlay**, born in 1930 in Stockton, California, is the champion of both disciplines who won gold medals at the 1956 and 1964 Olympics in the pair with coxswain event.

Named U.S. Rowings' Man of the Year in

2007, he was also part of the winning America's Cup sailing crews in 1974 and 1977.

From sport to medicine, **Carlos Finlay**, born in 1833 in Puerto Príncipe, Cuba, of Scottish and French ancestry, was the physician and scientist who pioneered research into the fatal yellow fever disease.

A graduate of the Jefferson Medical College in Philadelphia, Pennsylvania, he letter settled into medical practice in Havana.

In 1881, he was the first to theorise that mosquitoes were the carrier of yellow fever disease.

Chief Health Officer of Cuba from 1902 until six years before his death in 1915, and a member of Havana's Royal Academy of Medical, Physical and Natural Sciences, he was commemorated on a Cuban postage stamp issued in 1981.

In the contemporary legal world, **Donald Findlay** is the Queen's Counsel (QC) in Scotland who was born in 1951 in Cowdenbeath, Fife.

Recognised as Scotland's premier law advocate and elected chairman in 2010 of the Faculty of Advocates Criminal Bar Association, he is also a former vice-chairman of Rangers Football Club.

He has also been the subject of controversy

over incidents where he allegedly sang and told
sectarian jokes.

Bearers of the name have also left their
historical mark on the heavens.

This is through **William Henry Finlay**, born
in 1849 in Liverpool and who died in 1924.

He was first assistant at the Cape Observatory
in South Africa when, in September of 1866, he
discovered a periodic comet in the solar system that
was named *15P/Finlay* in his honour.